Women on Men

Great Quotations Publishing Company
Glendale Heights, Illinois

Compiled by Marlene Rimler
Cover Design . © Edna Lampke

© 1993 Great Quotations Publishing Company

Published in the United Stated by

Great Quotations Publishing Company,
1967 Quincy Court
Glendale Heights, Illinois 60139

Printed in Hong Kong
ISBN: 1-56245-040-9

The only time a woman really
succeeds in changing a man
is when he's a baby.

— Natalie Wood

"**B**oyfriends" weren't friends at all;
they were prizes, escorts,
symbols of achievement,
fascinating strangers, the other.

— Susan Allen Toth

It's not the men in my life that counts,
it's the life in my men.

— Mae West

A man in the house is worth
two in the street.

— Mae West

What's with you men?
Would hair stop growing on your chest
if you asked directions somewhere?

— Erma Bombeck

I want to know why, if men rule the world,
they don't stop wearing neckties.

— Linda Ellerbee

A fox is a wolf who sends flowers.

— Ruth Weston

I never married because there was no need.
I have three pets at home which answer
the same purpose as a husband.
I have a dog which growls every morning,
a parrot which swears all afternoon and a
cat that comes home late at night.

— Marie Corelli

A woman has got to love a bad man
once or twice in her life,
to be thankful for a good one.

— Marjorie Kinnan Rawlings

We had a lot in common,
I loved him and he loved him.

— Shelley Winters

A happy man marries the girl he loves,
but a happier man loves the girl he marries.

All men are liars, but some are not found
until after they are married.

A man finds it awfully hard to
lie to the woman he loves - the first time.

— Helen Rowland

Some women find it hard to tell a lie;
others can tell it as soon as
their husbands open their mouths.

It is always incompressible to a man
that a woman should refuse
an offer of marriage.

— Jane Austen

Wives are young men's mistresses,
companions for middle age,
and old men's nurses.

— Francis Bacon

A woman without a man is like
a fish without a bicycle.

— Gloria Steinem

Whatever women do they must do
twice as well as men to be
thought half as good.
Luckily, this is not difficult.

— Charlotte Whitton

I like men to behave like men.
I like them strong and childish.

— Francoise Sagan

I married beneath me, all women do.

— Nancy Astor

A husband always prefers his
wife's mother-in-law to his own.

'Tis my opinion every man cheats in his way,
and he is only honest who is not discovered.

— Susannah Centlivre

In passing, also I would like to say
that the first time Adam had a chance
he laid the blame on women.

— Lady Nancy Astor

Men have always detested women's gossip
because they suspect the truth:
Their measurements are being
taken and compared.

— Erica Jong

Whether women are better than men
I cannot say - but I can say
they are certainly no worse.

— Golda Meir

I never hated a man enough to
give him his diamonds back.

— Zsa Zsa Gabor

An archeologist is the best husband
a woman can have; the older she gets,
the more interested he is in her.

—Agatha Christie

One of the things about equality is
not just that you be treated equally to a man,
but that you treat yourself equally
to the way you treat a man.

— Marlo Thomas

A man has to be Joe McCarthy
to be called ruthless.
All a woman has to do is put you on hold.

— Marlo Thomas

When a man gets up to speak,
people listen, then look.
When a woman gets up, people look;
then, if they like what they see, they listen.

— Pauline Frederick

Whenever you want to marry someone,
go have lunch with his ex-wife.

— Shelley Winters

Personally, I think if a woman hasn't met
the right man by the time she's 24,
she may be lucky.

— Deborah Kerr

Sometimes I wonder if men and women
really suit each other.
Perhaps they should live next door
and just visit now and then.

— Katherine Hepburn

Show me a woman who doesn't feel guilty
and I'll show you a man.

— Erica Jong

I don't sit around thinking that I'd
like to have another husband;
only another man would
make me think that way.

— Lauren Bacall

When he is late for dinner and I know
he must be either having an affair
or lying dead in the street,
I always hope he is dead.

— Judith Viorst

Man forgives woman anything
save the wit to outwit him.

The best way to get most husbands
to do something is to suggest that
perhaps they're too old to do it.

— Shirley MacLaine

Men are taught to apologize
for their weaknesses,
women for their strengths.

— Lois Wyse

The best money advice ever
given me was from my father.
When I was a little girl, he told me,
"Don't spend anything unless you have to."

— Dinah Shore

I say I don't sleep with married men,
but what I mean is that I don't sleep
with happily married men.

— Britt Ekland

I won't say my previous husbands
thought only of my money,
but it had a certain fascination for them.

— Barbara Hutton

Marrying a man is like buying something
you've been admiring for a
long time in a shop window.
You may love it when you get it home,
but it doesn't always go
with everything else.

— Jean Kerr

I was never totally involved in movies.
I was making my father's dream come true.

— Mary Astor

I don't believe man is a
woman's natural enemy.
Perhaps his lawyer is.

— Shana Alexander

The characteristics that they criticize you for - that you are strong minded, that you make firm and tough decisions - are also characteristics which, if you were a man, they would praise you for.

— Margaret Thatcher

One cannot be always laughing at a man
without now and then
stumbling on something witty.

— Jane Austen

I like to wake up feeling a new man.

— Jean Harlow

Husbands are like fires.
They go out if unattended.

— Zsa Zsa Gabor

Trust your husband, adore your husband,
and get as much as you can
in your own name.

— Advice to Joan Rivers from her mother

If you want to sacrifice the admiration
of many men for the criticism of one,
go ahead, get married.

— Katharine Houghton Hepburn

Whenever I date a guy, I think,
is this the man I want my children
to spend their weekends with?

— Rita Rudner

Changing husbands is
only changing troubles.

— Kathleen Norris

'Tis the established custom (in Vienna)
for every lady to have two husbands,
one that bears the name and
another that performs the duties.

— Mary Wortley Montagu

I will feel equality has arrived when
we can elect to office women who are
as incompetent as some of the men
who are already there.

— Maureen Reagan

It isn't tying himself to one woman
that a man dreads when he thinks of marrying;
it's separating himself from all the others.

— Helen Rowland

Macho does not prove mucho.

— Zsa Zsa Gabor

Success has made failures of many men.

— Cindy Adams

If a man doesn't want a woman
to express her own opinions and be funny,
then he's not worth impressing.

— Carol Burnett

Men, their rights and nothing more;
Women, their rights and nothing less.

— Susan B. Anthony

The average man is more interested
in a woman who is interested in him
than he is in a woman, any woman,
with beautiful legs.

— Marlene Dietrich

If love means never having to say you're sorry,
then marriage means always having
to say everything twice.
Husbands, due to an unknown quirk of
the universe, never hear the first time.

— Estelle Getty

To be successful, a woman has to be
better at her job than a man.

— Golda Meir

Love will never be ideal until man recovers
from the illusion that he can be just
a little bit faithful or a little bit married.

— Helen Rowland

M en love with their eyes;
women love with their ears.

— Zsa Zsa Gabor

A man in love is incomplete
until he has married.
Then he is finished.

— Zsa Zsa Gabor

My husband wanted a room of his own:
He wanted it in Pittsburgh.

— Phyllis Diller

Men look at themselves in mirrors.
Women look at themselves.

— Elissa Melamed

My husband keeps saying, "Not tonight."
When I have a headache he hides the aspirin.

— Joan Rivers

To catch a husband is an art;
to hold him is a job.

— Mae West

Tell me why it is that every man
who seems attractive these days
is either married or barred on a technicality.

— Celeste Holm

Women want mediocre men,
and men are working hard to be
as mediocre as possible.

— Margaret Mead

Don't accept rides from strange men,
and remember that all men are strange as hell.

— Robin Morgan

Men are creatures with
two legs and eight hands.

— Jayne Mansfield

The trouble with some women is they
get all excited about nothing -
and then they marry him.

— Cher

If you want anything said, ask a man.
If you want anything done, ask a woman.

— Margaret Thatcher

When a girl marries she exchanges the
attentions of many men for
the inattention of one.

— Helen Rowland

The man I don't like doesn't exist.

— Mae West

I never loved a man I liked -
and never liked a man I loved.

— Fanny Brice

Μy message to men is:
"Don't screw around with women
because they can turn around
and screw you back."

— Jackie Collins

The best way to hold a man is in your arms.

— Mae West

Before marriage, a man will lie awake
all night thinking about something you said;
after marriage, he'll fall asleep
before you finish saying it.

— Helen Rowland

If a man watches three football games in a row,
he should be declared legally dead.

— Erma Bombeck

I only like two kinds of men:
domestic and imported.

— Mae West

The average secretary in the U.S.
is better educated than the average boss.

— Gloria Steinem

I'd like to get married because I like the
idea of a man being required by law
to sleep with me every night.

— Carrie Snow

Men are more conventional than women
and much slower to change their ideas.

— Kathleen Norris

First time you buy a house you see
how pretty the paint is and buy it.
The second time you look to see
if the basement has termites.
It's the same with men.

— Lupe Velez

Men say they love independence in a woman,
but they don't waste a second
demolishing it brick by brick.

— Candice Bergen

At my height, I'd like to boss
a group of men around.

— Carrie Fisher

I took up a collection for a man in our office.
But I didn't get enough money to buy one.

— Ruth Buzzi

Men often marry their mothers.

— Edna Ferber

Bigamy is having one husband too many.
Monogamy is the same.

— Erica Jong

For man, marriage is regarded as a station;
for women, as a vocation.

— Suzanne LaFollette

A husband is what is left of the lover
after the nerve has been extracted.

— Helen Rowland

My husband's going through mid-life crises.
He left me for an older woman!
What does she have that I don't,
except osteoporosis and orthopedic shoes?
If he would've waited ten years,
I could have given him those.

— Eileen Finney

A broken heart is what makes life
so wonderful five years later,
when you see the guy in an elevator
and he is fat and smoking a cigar
and saying long-time-no-see.
If he hadn't broken your heart,
you couldn't have that
glorious feeling of relief.

— Phyllis Battelle

I'm looking for a perfume to overpower men -
I'm sick of karate.

— Phyllis Diller

You never really know a man
until you have divorced him.

— Zsa Zsa Gabor

It's a man's world,
and you men can have it.

— Katherine Anne Porter

Before marriage, a girl has to
make love to her man to hold him;
after marriage, she has to hold him
to make love to him.

— Marilyn Monroe

Don't let a man put anything over you
except an umbrella.

— Mae West

He's the type of man who will end up
dying in his own arms.

— Miamie Van Doren on Warren Beatty

The only thing worse than a man
you can't control is a man you can.

— Margo Kaufman

There are far too many men in politics
and not enough elsewhere.

— Hermione Gingold

If the right man does not come along,
there are many fates far worse.
One is to have the wrong man come along.

— Letitia Baldrige

Can you imagine a world without men?
No crime and lots of happy fat women.

— Marion Smith

To a man, marriage means giving up
four out of five of the chiffonier drawers;
to a woman, giving up four
out of five of her opinions.

— Helen Rowland

A bachelor never quite gets over the idea
that he is a thing of beauty
and a boy forever.

— Helen Rowland

My Uncle Naibob wasn't a failure.
He just started out at the bottom
and liked it there.

— Minnie Pearl

To be a woman is to have the same
needs and longings as a man.
We need love and we wish to give it.

— Liv Ullmann

Man reaches the highest point of
lovableness at 12 to 17 -
to get it back, in a second flowering,
at the age of 70 to 90.

— Isak Dinesen

The hardest task in a girl's life is
to prove to a man that
his intentions are serious.

— Helen Rowland

A man's home may seem to be
his castle on the outside;
inside it is more often his nursery.

— Clare Booth Luce

If you never want to see a man again, say,
"I love you, I want to marry you.
I want to have children" -
they leave skid marks.

— Rita Rudner

Fighting is essentially a masculine idea;
a woman's weapon is her tongue.

— Hermione Gingold

A man may brave opinion;
a woman must submit to it.

— Anna Louise De Stael

Women speak because they wish to speak,
whereas a man speaks only when driven
to speech by something outside himself -
like, for instance, he can't find any clean socks.

— Jean Kerr

Whatever you may look like,
marry a man your own age -
as your beauty fades, so will his eyesight.

— Phyllis Diller

He has so many muscles that he has
to make an appointment to move his fingers.

— Phyllis Diller (on Arnold Schwatzenegger)

I go for tough, uncommunicative guys
who ride motorcycles.

— Ally Sheedy

I love being married. It's so great to find
that one special person you want to
annoy for the rest of your life.

— Rita Rudner

There are only two kinds of men -
the dead and the deadly.

— Helen Rowland

I refuse to consign the whole male sex
to the nursery. I insist on believing that
some men are my equals.

— Brigid Brophy

When men reach their sixties and retire,
they go to pieces.
Women go right on cooking.

— Gail Sheehy

Great men are not always idiots.

— Karen Elizabeth Gordon

If they could put one man on the moon,
why can't they put them all?

— Unknown

The fantasy of every Australian man
is to have two women -
one cleaning and the other dusting.

— Maureen Murphy

Burt Reynolds once asked me out.
I was in his room.

— Phyllis Diller

He's the kind of man a woman would
have to marry to get rid of.

— Mae West

There is so little difference
between husbands
you might as well keep the first.

— Adela Rogers St. Johns

Dear boy, it isn't that your manners are bad -
it's simply that you have no manners at all.

— Margot Asquith

Lord Birkenhead is very clever,
but sometimes his brains go to his head.

— Margot Asquith

I wouldn't trust my husband with a young woman for five minutes, and he's been dead for 25 years.

— Brendan Behan's mother

Never marry a man who can't please you.
If you'd rather be with someone else,
then don't make the commitment.

— Dr. Joyce Brothers

My mother said: "Marry a man with
good teeth and high arches."
She thought I should get that into
the genetic structure of the family.

— Jill Clayburgh

I am a marvelous housekeeper.
Every time I leave a man I keep his house.

— Zsa Zsa Gabor

He's the kind of man who
picks his friends - to pieces.

— Mae West

The more I see of man, the more I like dogs.

— Mme de Stael

Why does a woman work ten years
to change a man's habits
and then complain that he's
not the man she married.

— Barbara Streisand

After an acquaintance of ten minutes
many women will exchange confidences
that a man would not reveal
to a lifelong friend.

— Page Smith

I have found men who didn't
know how to kiss.
I've always found time to teach them.

— Mae West

Plain women know more about men
than beautiful ones do.

— Katharine Hepburn

I don't need a man to rectify my existence.
The most profound relationship
we'll ever have is the one with ourselves.

— Shirley MacLaine

A bachelor is a man
who is right sometimes.

A woman is a woman until the day she dies,
but a man's a man only as long as he can.

— Moms Mabley

The best husbands aren't caught,
they're made.

There are two kinds of husbands:
Those who never talk back to their wives,
and those who listen
in an aggravating manner.

A woman never knows what kind
of a husband she doesn't want
until she marries him.

Every girl waits for the right man
to come along, but in the meantime
she gets married.

Behind every man who achieves success
stands a mother, a wife and the IRS.

— Ethel Jacobson

Women, it's true, make human beings,
but only men can make men.

— Margaret Mead

What is the use of being a little boy
if you are going to grow up to be a man.

— Gertrude Stein

My ancestors wandered lost in the wilderness for 40 years because even in biblical times, men would not stop to ask for directions.

— Elayne Boosler

Poor little men! Poor little strutting peacocks!
They spread out their tails as conquerors
almost as soon as they are able to walk.

— Jean Anouilh

As long as you know that
most men are like children,
you know everything.

— Coco Chanel

If there is anything disagreeable going on,
men are sure to get out of it.

— Jane Austen

There's nothing so stubborn as a man
when you want him to do something.

— Jean Giraudoux

A woman's virtue is
man's greatest invention.

— Cornelia Otis Skinner

All the men on my staff can type.

— Bella Abzug

I don't know why women want any of the things men have when one of the things that women have is men.

— Coco Chanel

I have no hostility towards men.
Some of my best friends are men.
I married a man, and my father was a man.

— Jill Ruckelshaus

It takes two women to raise one male -
his mother and his wife.

The great truth is that
women actually like men,
and men can never believe it.

— Isabel Patterson

The trouble with men is that
they're too much alike,
and the trouble with women
is that they aren't.

OTHER TITLES BY GREAT QUOTATIONS PUBLISHING COMPANY

GREAT QUOTATIONS PUBLISHING CO.

1967 Quincy Court

Glendale Heights, IL 60139-2045

Phone (708) 582-2800

FAX (708) 582-2813